Rapturous Chronicles

Rapturous Chronicles

Judith Fitzgerald

The Mercury Press

ACKNOWLEDGEMENTS

I am indebted to Daniel Jalowica for his constant support and guidance and to
Beverley Daurio for her encouragement.

Without the aid of a Canada Council A Grant, a Toronto Arts Council Research and
Development Grant, and Ontario Arts Council Writers' Reserve funds via Black Moss Press,
Canadian Fiction Magazine, The Canadian Forum, Cross-Canada Writers' Quarterly,
The Mercury Press, Penumbra Press, This Magazine, and Williams-Wallace Publishing,
this book would not exist. Thank you.

"Shine a Light on Me, Operator : Get Me Jesus on the Line" first appeared in
Canadian Fiction Magazine; "East of West Crescent," and "Moon, a Lantern, and a Collar"
first appeared in paragraph; "Lacuna : Luna Sea" first appeared in Orbis.

§

The publisher gratefully acknowledges the financial assistance
of the Canada Council and the Ontario Arts Council.

Cover design: Gordon Robertson
Author photograph: Avrum Fenson
Production co-ordination: The Blue Pencil
Typeset in Goudy Old Style and Gill Sans by TASK. Printed and bound in Canada.

Canadian Cataloguing in Publication:

Main entry under title:
Fitzgerald, Judith, 1952–
Poems.
ISBN 0-920544-82-7
I. Title
PS8561.I88R3 1991   C811'.54   C91-094569-1
PR9199.3.F5R3 1991

_____

Canadian Sales Representation: The Literary Press Group.

The Mercury Press is distributed in Canada
by University of Toronto Press,
and in the United States
by Inland Book Company (selected titles)
and Bookslinger.

The Mercury Press
(an imprint of Aya Press)
Box 446
Stratford, Ontario
Canada N5A 6T3

CONTENTS

Note : *the room / one narrow world / that might be anywhere...*
&
Key :

alibi alpha apple atlantic azalea
barrazza baseball bilabial bravo broken
camera chaos civilisation completion content cross
death delta diamond direction drift
echo energy envelope everglades
fabrication façade family form foxtrot frame
garden geography glass guitar gulf
heartache her / hymn history hotel humilitas hurricane
ice immolation imprint india intercession
jasmine Jesus
key knife knot knowledge
lacunae ladder language line love
memory miami mirage moon mouth music mystery myth
narrative nashville night november
oasis october olson omega oxymoron
persona phenom poetics pornography projectilliant
québec question
refuge reparation requiem reunion
sacrifice serpent south station synchronicity
tango technique telegram toronto train
umbrella unguardian universe
vacuum vang velocity voice
walleye water weather western window
x Xtian
yellow yesterday you / yours
zed zeliotrope zero zone

In Memory of Juan Butler (4 July 1942 – 2 June 1981)

"... In this respect, criticism is not only a system
of notation and categorization — it is an active
and definitive engagement with what a text proposes... "
— Robert Creeley, "Introduction," *Selected Writings of Charles Olson*

O western wind when wilt thou blow,
And the small rain down shall rain
O Christ that my love were in my arms
And I in my bed again

Woman, Language Made Me

Where I come from, I learn myself into existence by reading words
in newspapers. We own no books. Too young to go to school. Then
The Toronto Star boxes come at Christmas and each of us kids receives
a remaindered copy of something or other. None of the cousins, brothers,
boarder's children, or sisters reads or wants to read books. I begin my tiny
library then, at three. Only two books, however, remain in my memory.
One book, although I read it until its bookness and title dissolve and
I remember the way it looks as a book, makes no sense at all. The other,
I recall only too well : *How to Raise Rabbits.*

Names and origins and etymology all add up to the same thing for me.
I can't see peeling a name from the thing named. I can't hear taking
a place out of a place placed. My fascination with language or,
as Fraser Sutherland astutely calls it, my love affair with language,
stems from precisely these notions. My mother was born of a Swedish
mother and a Parisien father; my father was born of a Québécoise mother
and a Québécois father. That makes me one-quarter Swedish, one-quarter
Parisienne, and half-Québécoise with an Irish name. Before I
discover this, I suffer from the Irish curse, alcoholism. When I learn no
Irish blood flows in me, I look at my options. I haven't touched a drop
since. I believe in the power of language, of names, of etymology, of origin.
Others believe in the power of AA.

I feel so close to everything we've lost; we'll never, never have to

Where I come from, in short, books do not exist. Language as an instrument of dialogue does not exist. What does exist is my mother, a grade-six reform-school dropout. When I was born, my mother was going on 18. And my uncle, a bit younger than my mother, a charmer, a baseball pitcher for the Toronto Maple Leafs, a lover of language. On Saturdays, he picks us up to watch him play ball. On the way to and from games, he drills me.

Where I come from, I learn to read by letters on billboards, street signs, and score cards. Baseball score cards. I like baseball. I love baseball. My uncle, I learn years later, does not pitch nearly as well as he (and I) think/s he does. And language? Functionally illiterate.

The letters in POWER'S SUPERMARKET, SIMON DE GROOT'S, MAPLE LEAF GARDENS, and TAMBLYN'S DRUGSTORE : My first introduction to language. Some of the stores still line Church Street. In an odd or even twist of fate, one of them carries an incredible number of baseball titles, THIS AIN'T THE ROSEDALE LIBRARY.

Books banned, really, in my natural mother's house; we move every other month and they weigh too much. My obsession with the alphabet, with language, accelerated through reading *The Toronto Star* and *Telegram*. I love the stories, the columns, Ann Landers, Dear Abby, the type, the headlines, even the obituaries which I still habitually read (when a newspaper drifts into my home on the wing of a visitor).

Yet, the words, the language keeps me going, the world I create from words and wrap around me. Each new word tastes and smells and feels itself into my nervous system. Sounded over and over, each becomes exotic bird, flower, place. Each provides transport. Words such as *diaphanous, inchoate, gardenia,* my cause for reflection and assimilation shimmering in my head. Knowledge : A look.

---

lose it again. She avoids linear logic, east-west trajectory, fixed axis

I want them all, their stories, the stories they suggest. My language, from newspapers to Cabbagetown mangle, makes me the woman I am, provides me with safe passage through delinquent childhood, arrested adolescence, incarcerated adulthood. This woman. This language. If I break down, we dissolve together. I stand before you and defy imagination, inclination, inspiration, information — all the *I* s looking out.

The oldest question, the one about desert-island strands. The look of paradise in your eyes tonight.   I'll wake up below deck in hot morning haze. Fix impromptu ledgers. Make the best of a western situation. Which book would you take and all? A blank one. Make it my own, my own language. *gonna walk away from trouble / with my head held high / then look closer / you'll see luck in my eyes*

Where I come from, just beyond the familiar building / horizon line I believe will not change, everything changes. From wood to concrete. I learn memory and motion, do not read backs of cereal boxes, learn laws and rules. The way a crane will hold a steel girder. The way a hand will crush a soft shoulder. The way an arm can break so easily. How to know the true and distinguish it from truth; how to lie, mostly down, rarely up to scratch. [Eddie C. put spikes in the tires of the car.]

I keep a close watch on this heart of mine. I stand in a kitchen with my natural mother in the late Fifties — before Crown Wardship in the house of the Province of Ontario. She sits by the old walnut radio playing Johnny Cash, Elvis Presley, and Patti Page; balances both cigarette and coffee cup in her right hand. She seems old to me. Tired. She seems irretrievable, not yet creasing into her thirties. *Are you sorry we drifted apart?*

---

of a hot blue star.   Satellite sister, a cool white revolution while he,

She says a social worker will "come to get youse kids." The basement-apartment kitchen feels damp, pale yellow. I want to know why. She says she's tired of kids. I tell her how wrong she is to give us away and how sorry she will be when I make a million dollars as a writer. It doesn't faze her. *Cross over the bridge.*

I know the essential element; it takes me almost thirty-five years to believe, to trust, to celebrate, to utter the most difficult phrase in my language : I am a writer. Language then, says me, this woman, the key and cornerstone of self, of existence. The only inhuman aspect to matters of absolutely human face.

I cannot think beyond the concept of eternity because I do not possess language for such thinking... I immediately rankle. Scientists may not possess such a language, but in order to imagine beyond limitations, horizons, borders, or eternities, we need only to turn to language turned beyond the blue neon.

Street, I think, or road. As good a place as any. Streets and roads lead where and here — what? Sounds of the street. Rules of the road. The way. *In the beginning...* Say instead, try tongue on, in the *being* and the circle makes more circles, crescents, moons. In the being, the word, the sun in morning, moon at his feet, the road a warning, the siren a street. NO! Sun at her feet as well.

Pick a word. This word : Layer, not layered. Out of thin air, context, time, space, and in the road (though off the street). Layer, or cakewalk. Can she bake an apple... Could HE? And then think *tree,* itself, part of the way. That core towards existence. Yes, I see, hear, know the S.

Layer always leads to layers and etymology and all that resonance.

---

brazen sun, imagines him self centred. *"It is the sudden, harsh,*

Okay. Layer. Fill of S. But S [bless S house], she knows a road when she walks one. Where went she away. Past tree, essence. Layers of blankets, sheets, this journey to understand S in the street. Fill it in. Short form.

[In the being : The word. The word wrote a number : For a good time, call. Lowly. Sweetly. Form, any minute. Walking streetly. *The first one does the talking.*]

In the being the word said : Let there be S . And S spoke up right smartly : You bet yer sweet S I will!

Rode, I think. S did. This : Where the cowgirl rides away. But how do we know that? Boys boys, sure; cows cows. But cowgirls don't hang around the old corral. A man may work from sun to sun, but a woman's writing's never undone, moonface. Rode. E. O. Rode /o. The point? Simply that cowgirls *n'existent pas.*

Word, to unit, to phoneme, to sound, to source and source squared. To take the word, to de-complicate it, to break it open and look inside. To start from the word and look up to see the moon. And then, ride 'em, woman of the wildest West. Est. 1952 Inc. beneath jet-black beams of darkness. Wilderness. Es equals Os. O*u/est* equals Western standard line.

Women and Language. I excise the "&" or "and." Ampersand, connective tissue of re/written history. I re/write history. Nitpicker? Probably. I re/lease language; my one & only human refuge, statelessness of being. Impenetrable. Language made me. No complaints. Ecologic body sound gyno/sense, neither violated nor dis/graced. (Amazing Dis/grace : *I once was found, but now I'm learning.*)

---

glaring realisation that hidden, unfriendly eyes have been following

This road, that street, the way.   Line of language, the lineup.   Top
of the order, bottom of the eighth, Octavio!   I cannot resist.   I stand
helpless before her.   Mine.   A line, linear, lineage lateral.   I claim it.
You claim it.   She claims me.

[He who traditionally misses the difference between claimant and owner
cannot, of course.]   Why we continue — Being. — precise ways.

A singular noun   :   Languiture.   Here, the space to speech.

Speak / sound.   Over and in.   Look ma, no excuses!   Or a line from

a country song : *I've got swinging doors, a jukebox, and a barstool.*

My new home has a flashing neon sign.   Now, why did I write this?

How many miles to the gallon to Babylon?   You get the drift,

continental?

Vancouver
May 1988

---

your every movement, violating the privacy of your ecstasy."

**Once
in a Blue Moon**

What can I possibly tell you, tellurium? Cartographer of strict
and punctual direction : I only know the lines between the lines
by heart, by sight, by these malfunctioning impulses leading
to an impossible map. All day, the touch of hands dreams faces, lines,
shadows, travels through fingers to erupt in fine light language. Sweet
need imprinted, *imprimaturs*, impulsive, rare. Heat rising, faith waning.
I find your centre — exquisite imbedded shapes and spaces indwelling —
where Angelology ignites. Expansive vocabulary, expanding night.
Spreading wide wings, you soar drenched, flame immanent.
Imagining more. A conflagration : Irreducible given.

His death occurred at the moment of conception. A long-stemmed

You hold open familiar doors, capture extraordinary angles of light.
Enthralled, I see your cauterised world in tender relief, see it through
the window of your exquisite faith. Body, poetic, holy rite of palliation.
The dark magnitude, the darker misgivings. Earth to flesh to earth.
And then, heart, a blossoming anodyne. We went out with the weather,
pale moon floating above our heads, a melodious white, an enduring

star, charming in its familiarity. Evening starling blue. Walking. Liquid
haze of friendship gauze almost, shimmering in a cellophane cocoon.
We spent the evening gently, dreaming present tense. And beneath
the ring of white, sheer weight of self-destruction smouldering in bright
circles, declining light. Enough. The passion we fathom beyond.
Long-distance teardrops in slant diagonal light. Leaning against

the condensed window, recalling mornings, grey, sullen, surfaced.
A coffin of need of detachment. Terse attenuations, windows and tears
and remains infiltrated. The masc(u)line. It's late; sea-glass window
shades drawn over evening; low light suffused with subterranean vision.
At this exquisite feminine juncture words intersect with sapphire layers
of night. Evening arises from the silk handkerchief, from *blue moon*

over heartache. Dictatorship a memory. Oppressed by the Catalonian
sense of rigour. Labyrinthian and lost. Narrow streets. Hallowed signs.
Deterioration of façades, an elegant urban backdrop, gentle contaminations.
Fog hangs over the city, an atmospheric given. Barcelona lies
with her back to the sea. The truth :
I'm always on a mountain when I fall.

---

liaison. *A new covenant in his blood.* Agonising in the flesh, patterned

Prison still exists in each carbon trace of his body; synaptic obsolescence not engendered by planes of proof. You exist beyond existence and fill in the blanks. Play dead or Monopoly. Listen to the siren claiming, re-claiming, self beyond sonority. You turn me over in your thoughts and I tumble through imaginary hands. A grand passion grief etches in the first

person. Languid, urgent : The oxymoron of love. Or death. On the healing cusp of a broken heart. In harmony of moonlight, driving again. Strips of gibbous memory float above the expressway and drift off into the horizon. Pale evening star heightened to black through shimmering reflection of your past. You turn to look in the sideview

mirror and disappear. The image shatters, approaches glassy concurrence. Synonymous combustion of self and other. Your hands still float above the tree line, green line of shade and breathing. I reflect upon that evening on the balcony. Leaning into the city. Suspension. Bridged between yesterday and this brick wall, spinning in the vortex of fish and line

and sinking. Death by dreaming. I am not nothing without you. But I still wear t/his cowboy hat, still two-step with the moon. Okay. I shall change my name and forget the sadness and sorrow, shall break down the beauty I once believed. And all this grace and grief, private intersections in the far reaches of an infinitely broken heart. Even these trophies of

a life well-intentioned catch in the net of despair. A great beating of wings challenges the silent anguish of my inner ear. I shall change my name, seek sanctuary in the hollow language you insist I undress, lie down, spread my conscious despair across these utterly dead icons of the linguistic self. Okay. You may call me anyone. Or albatross.

---

on a dying civilisation; Paschal Mystery raised up in unaffected blood.

Alphabet and phoneme, cuts of this condition fan out in albatross aberration, water care. Carbon consonants create these curved and careful digressions from liquid to sky where, according to discord, mariners gather to discuss the perils of beauty. And fishing.

REASON : The graceless whore who blows a sibilant and suggests logic resides in extreme rigidity. And, at its core, the apple supports precise kinds of suppression.

EMOTION : The thorn in your heart, bloodied outline, a slash through tears. Another time. Another place. Another key. Occurs anywhere. But here. Here, the temporal indifference to waterlilies breaks my heart.

You, me, whatever, for extemporaneous now, to dwell unconsciously lost in things, such words we cannot hear, cannot separate moon from madness, art from atmosphere, the implication of gardens. This inhuman race, hopeless causeway we travel and return, circle, encircle, enfold,

seal to saurian cycle, close to self to suffocation. The dagger of dreams, the amnesty of other staked through the heart. Tonight, country-music clear, a chrysalis of familiarity, I think of you unaccustomed to three-quarter time, the night we found a kind of honkytonk heaven, how you

drove that moon-weathered strip, evening. To give over : I tend towards endlessly empty hands, my eyes blind and my albatross inscribed. Take this from the heart : My everlasting alphabetic gallows.
I'm down to my last cigarette.

Your cheap violin and your cross. Imprimi Potest. The stations : Xtian.

Full Moon

I wanted to divide myself in two [my self : ju an] but beep's poem:
em ty

Eloquently.   I started seeing shadows in the corners of love/d letters.
When I fell, I fell spectacularly.   Evening news.   Marconi blues.   I give,

gave, go over the rim, the long black truth in this exquisitely perfected hell.
The maddening absence.   Moon : Full.   Heart : Empty.

To elevate the irretrievable mass and extract the distillant implications
of a heart shattered through mission, daily memory.   *Rex caelestis...*

I'll let you wear my cowboy hat.   We sat at a red-chequered table devising
divisions of memory loss and lost.   For a time (and a place) we believed

the trouble with identity erupted in natural sequence, a logical procession
of names. Adopt-a-self, so to speak.   Yet the act engendered only another

visa to negotiate the land-mine of time not time.   Structure introduces
order.   *This is where the cowboy rides away.*

How we both wrapped ourselves in the same cut of fabric — protection
against knives and scissors, the beautiful fragile thread of hunger private

and vulnerable.   What we wanted to understand we knew intuitively.
We sprawled on the edges of a large life, larger hurt, caught anger and

---

I call to you, I call to you, but I don't call soft enough.   (Optional Our

anguish in the parameters of extreme love.   There.   I said this and this
and that.   I wanted you and eventually completely broke down in wanting

you.   Or allowed you to break me down and eventually you did.   My fault,
my fault, my most grievous fault?   One.   But that dusts the surface of bone

through ulterior dependence.   Hurricane fodder, the annihilation of other.
Journey past afternoon to beat of cotton heart.   It's always Juan in these

fine sheets, onion skin, retroflex opportunity to view the ashes of his
terrified soul. It hurled me into the eye of blood / vision, idea and

its memory.   No warmth but lots of heat.   These private excursions
through our deeply moving hell, two halves of a heart, a binary flotilla

of horrors.   I renamed to *either*; he opted for *or*.   Through self-
abnegation he arrived (departed) gracelessly.   He entered me and,

battery acid succinct / efficient, produced energy to overthrow, over
come, destroy the vast and aching vacuum of self.   Not the raw, exposed

extremities of our hearts, the nerve endings, severings, electrical impulses
burned into our fingers, psalms, handouts.   Some pamphlets for disaster

we learn intuitively; some formal considerations under pressure fall
and fall. Haunts. And yes, the ghost of all ghosts we bring to each moment,

movement, moratorium on fear.   Some songs brook no music :
Could it be somebody lied?   Others hold each strand of silence,

each semi-tone of quiet. How I wish, for cruel example, you lived,
I relived. The error imprinted on my life, your death, our collusion.

Father, Hail Mary, Glory be to the Father.)   Pilate passing sentence.

No melody can reproduce the exchange of condemnatory vows.
Nor its specific location in Angiography.

The door to this prison hangs open.   I do time proving the subjectivity
of guilt and grace.   Juan, hold me bone close and blind these unforgiving

honkytonk visions.   I do this :   Believe you, believe you took your life
in some celebration of autonomy.   Painful light.

a region religion reigns in. a returning. turning / return the lovers.

East of West Crescent

Heartless night.   No language I intuit does justice and although I come
to an agreement with meaning *per se,* I still seek the unseekable,
the unspeakable, the forbidden page containing pure signs and symbols,
keys and coda, heart and healing.   But — conjunction — it only matters
because I alleviate the after images, the shadows, the ghosting effects of
his psychic narrative response. Forget the fiction of fact, the truth of myth.
Truth : Stranger for fiction (even when you fabricate it).   *Don't call him
a cowboy unless you seen him ride.*   Out of reach, range, radio.

Lost in a strand of aqueous desire, an ironic interdirectional curve
against self. Sinking into / pulling away :   Hell and historical imperative.
Focus and redemption   :   The rhythm maudlin, the urge banal.   Amniotic
inquest a fruitless construction, no destination in metonymous scrutiny.
The friction of fact. *Historical,* a private pure sense. Ah, yes. Bless this
moment, saturant with clarity, second-sight vision.   Easy to turn (three-
quarter time) and dissolve.   Thin coating vs thick skin.   All this pushes
itself against the wall of my left / right ventricle, of my heart's constant

collision.   Complete to the thickness of this fault line, this precarious crust
and the notes of salt symphonies, redolent with some language I learned
after you took your life into your own.   I never believed in the danger of
gathering stars, of reparation. I write in brilliant darkness, in the exquisite
chaos of true gravity, listen to "Heart Like Mine" and hold my breath until
the voice reaches the end of our intertwined line of, field of, range of
precision.   I write for you, for the sheerest palest green exuberance you
jubilantly embraced. Universal amputation. Hemispheres of sorrow.

And no regret, rebel heart, *nada.*

Seed of condemnation planted in the garden of a suburban and mani-

I took you
for love.

*By your
own hand.*

Tonight, tangible, less than evening, always the eye, the hand, what keeps
beating under a jaundiced moon.   Clouds of dead reckoning cover the slant
sky with reinforced steel.   A search through memories to meaning, under-
standing, under moon light splashes awash in flesh.

Por el amor de Dios, ayudeme Usted, que mi hijito tiene hambre.

Letters equal a body of work in this instance, the alphabet, corpus yet
pagan.   Blossoming into silence.   Undressing language, defusing one's skin,
rescinding cellular composition.   Incongruence by the number.   Numbers
by the score.   *When the phone don't ring you'll know it's me.*   An open
phone.   I collide with the distance long past.   Attract an absolute.
Geography affects the story.   Necessity, not of faith, but of linguistic
latitude and longitude, the essential place of place.   Abstraction   :
It wouldn't be so bad if it hadn't been so good.

We all struggle to make a mark.   In the story he fires a gun.   *Adios
Canadiense.*   The butler polishes the goblets.   The bullets hit High C.
Everything shatters.   Molecules of gunpowder fill atoms of distress.
An operatic conclusion to a fate worse than fate.

Adios.

Adios.

---

cured intelligence.   *I'll bury my soul in a scrapbook.*   I'll keep moving.

Moon, a Lantern, and a Collar

And still : A passive-verb night in the middle of my life. Sitting
in the Queen's Dairy on St. Clair Avenue West I hear a voice across
the tables above the scratching needle :

There is one moment... one moment in your life when everything...

I turn to see. Past Last Call with two bottles of Molson's Golden before him.
Face scarred and hands incoherent with trembling, six feet tucked into
tiny blue corner. Scarf of Stewart Clan and Macdonald's Export between
lips. Inhaling. (I reflect upon the coincidence.) Reflection glazing beer-
smeared eyes. Native of these parts. Fostering analects by terse
association. The alveolar sentence. He repeats *moment* and says nothing

more. Exhales across the room, a smoke-laden sigh. The table sags; his
chair fatigues. I turn but he disappears in succinct sentence. We both
know this moment; both seek utter completions. Moment. This moment.
Synchronicity. My life encoded in the way I respond to an otherwise
invisible drunk on the far side of hell. It changes nothing. He recedes in
the aural landscape of poverty and exhilaration. I play poker for a living.
Make concessions to supply and demand. Pay taxes. Smoke too much.
Writing is an insurmountable fiction, an estranged perspective on the act
of approximation by appropriation. Juan lived by proximity in the hard

---

Juan begins a course punctuated by suffering and learns to take the

heart of it; died at its feet, a secular death hardened by the exigencies
of casting out snakes, demons in his garden of grief. He pulled the trigger
on the novel : The only way he believed he could end it. An eye for
an eye. A truth for a truth. This requires neither talent nor poetry.
I arrive here through the back door and leave by the late-night light
of a thousand exits. Method corrected, leave taking another step
in the radical editorial process. Moment by moment. Turn away from
one, fall back into self, source, wall. The space where head and heart
collide in local time these endlessly wounded days.

I write this, late, later. One eye on the clock and one ear on *The History
of Country Music.* *I don't know whether to kill myself or go bowling.*
Want to make it beautiful but realise the vocabulary for beauty I once
possessed belongs in a dictionary of need I need no longer. *Ablaze with
beauty.* Yes. A purple heart, amaranth blood. Red moments. Haggard,
always on a mountain :

> *I hate to say I'm giving up
> but I believe losing's just become
> a way of life with me.*

If I could capture that moment this, somehow deal with its indelibility,
explain to someone something, anything. One thing. A pair of jacks,
aces high. The jackpot, king pin, queen petrified. I hear "El Paso" on
the radio and a trillium of faces blooms in retrospect. Juan, Juan, Juan.
All the more. And reasons. He remains t/here, indented, grey hair wild
and hands stilled. We both laugh in the face of another vast night.
An insurmountable fiction.
Adios.
Adios.

---

cross literally. *I've loved you all my life. That's how I want to end it.*

27

Flat-Top Moon Gothic

Dreamscape into your circle of longing, your imperfect need enough now.
I know the limits / limitations of your hands.   Tonight my nostalgia equals
my need of you; I forgive everything because it means so little in the grand
central scheme of pain (and I conjure up your sense so often I imagine
time spatially irrelevant).   A simple situation.   Beyond itself
in the kitchen window night tethered to microscopic mutations,
an almost photographic composition, a superimposed present / future.
The transubstantiation of grace.   I emerge : A camera.   Reel back
instant frames from the front.   The splendid hunter's moon.

The way you always spoke my name with pure indifference.
Incarcerated heart.   Immoral seed.   The various levels of heaven.
Again.   Middle night, middle life vs class and strict scripture.   Against
the flutter of evening I wake to write the wrong / doings and comings
and goings and cannot wait for ever [for always dissolves] and the quest
formulation (mutation) rears post-woman.   The achievement of zero.
  The way to break down, rend, a demolition expert —
Just a moment.   A building here.
  — upon this moment.   Space.   Self.   Needs.   Fill.

The riddle of suffering and the mystery of our human condition deeply

If I say such (timbre of voice) and so on. The idea tears me
apart at the seams, body / mind split.   Wholesale slaughter of self
and story raises the central, the grand central zero upon which
a certain facsimile of self exists in the world, nervous system.
To sight language, see its sheen in white mornings, immutable.
Self-generated, self-gendered.   Woman.   *Woman burns with imagination.*
From this moment, expiate the investiture of skin, reinvent,
without antecedent, precedent, parallel / holograph/ic muse   :
Bond, owner and claimant (*amantes*), neither lust nor found.

Aspirant, bilabial affliction, the binary of each cast/e,
off words, restore, re/story, population, punctuation. Always,
the core, my apple c/art. Period.   Less, in the impulse,
in the pulsing spaces between root and utterance, each tendril
horizontal, act and artifact, cartography of skin.   Exquisite moments
of ecstasy and communion and the need for saturation.   Now I must
transform myself, this self, feminine body and spirit, into self you
embody, empower.   I en/courage, take flight in order to dwell
in your arms   :   Extenuate male circumstance.   Spirit / flesh,

self contained in seed, love's four corners, two bands, no contest.

This unholy alliance, my pure wedding in the alphabetic disclosure,
a moratorium on the declension of *serpentes et échelles.*
Strip to core, apple, flesh, seed of language, the buried voice
I articulate, an article of faith, of fiction, story of us,
two halves of anoetic music, an unceremonious whole.
We could always go out dancing, kick up our heels against
low-flying clouds of superstition, of bleached weather.
The home key was the anchorage, the safe harbour,
the foreign key represented adventure.

---

stir our hearts and spoil our happiness here on earth.   Ice Station Zero.

Running interference on the woman I know from far too many angles;
see in clarity her hand movements, her tiny adjustments / readjustments
to something in the air — music or longing — or the minutiae of self-
meaning where alignments and realignments recur and recombine
in the distracted way she pushes white through strands of crescent hair,
gathering it in, absconding night and terrible blackness enfolding flesh.
Being. This business of going on, gerunds and all, these endings. Light and
shadow rise together this evening, early warning signs of life muffled
by sheer brooding line of sky beyond waterslash, treestreak, keyhaven.

Dusk. Velvet. Crimson. Your attention unravels, counterpoints delicious
recollection. Wrapt attraction. Rapturous chronicles of evening.
Juan, let us remain ancient and passionate, forgive impossible histories,
forget the future monochromatic. Midnight and sadness. Double
syllabic count. Who listens? Still black night a shawl under which I
huddle, an umbrella against need (inexpressible) and grief (unexplainable).
A dream, really, an adverbial aside. Complicated and blue. Juan,
we work at cross purposes; we break our hearts. Language the record
and repository of extreme unction. Words accumulate against

the inevitable reckoning, the temporal demands of heart and shadow.
I   bear   down.
Starboard to centreboard, telltale to the wind.   Dazzle me, anchoring array
of start and shore, combustion of lightning, salutation of self.   Arrival,
departure, wrench heart, halyard.   The corruption of angels, the contra-
bandana of the executioner's hymn.   Cannot look into eye, caught sun
squared. Always lacked winch, shroud, vang.   Wore Titanium whites,
gazebo reds, inkblack blues.   Shackled.   Implication of garland and rings.
Fairlead to home. Cutter evening. Level on the level. Port. Slashed sails.

Life produces casualties of absence and sorrow : Transubstantiation.

Waning Reflexive

Juan, I want you in a way I want nothing else, other, *double entendre.*
To here, this moment.   Ten years ago you walked into some kitchen
and sat tentatively by the window, waiting for a signal, keeping counsel
with the starling in the garden.   You put your feet on cumulus hold
while stratospheric emotions trailed in unison.   Your huge (it seems) hands
open, voice closing, eyes already glazed with despair.   Juan, Juan,
where did you come from?   Vancouver or hell.   Wafers and cheap wine.
An aura you planned to leave behind.   I wanted to replace the pen,
remove the desolation, absorb the odour of death.   Then or there,

in the moving fiction, in the resumption of work.   The pen you left here
left carelessly.   I saw the transformation of azaleas, the marked petals
in moonlight splinters, the hands helpless and scar/r/ed.   I wanted
the touch of your awful mortality, the exaltation of host and guest.
You wanted amnesia and wood.   Dreamer, you recalled a time
(in archetype and symbol), a time when language had not taken its toll.
Spoke of the wheel slicing through fiction; spoke of the impossibility
of art.   Mimesis, it dawned on you, and took you to dusk.   Too difficult
to bear the art we ex/tr/act.   Rivulets of a deeply wounded world.

Remember the typewriter?   Of all things, inanimate.   So näive, such
cheap romanticism.   I believed it talismanic, the missing omen.
Spluttering talent and concentrated oppression.   I contributed :
To reap, to return, to roil.   You found haphazard starlight, believed you
could never approximate pure grief, sat by the dissolving frame and
watched the window disappear.   I wanted you fixed, writerly, your
image untarnished.   Some ribbon and a handful of keys.   I returned
to my fantasies, parched gardens, the bird with the broken wing.
But you out-dreamed the definition, Juan; you ran ahead of the frame.

Ariadne auf Naxos.   Picks up slivers in obscure stations, radio country.

What happened to the pawn ticket? Fiction will never be the same.
An iconographic set of interior apprehensions : A ring of keys, a glass
of time, a door of flesh when

BUTLER, Juan – Suddenly at Toronto

I return, unravel, know only this shadowed guilt, put self before other,
want to fall through light. I no longer traverse, transgress. I allowed
the suicide in his eyes. I broke the rhythm of his breath. He stares down
the barrel of his own devising; puts the end in his mouth and releases
the safety catch. He tightens the knots and severs the ties. The knife
myriads in flesh; the sound breaks its own barriers, muffles into madness.

These ashes, this replica, that facsimile, the ghosting film of closing time.
I wanted need, epiphany of desire, small acts of exhilaration. He believed
passion could not correlate itself in the grand scheme of things. Kept to
the third person, alternate persona, locked it out. When he took his life
to the edge of morning, I went with. Angles and planes of language
collide in the skin of death, in the sin of love. I arrive at this moment
[in the past], set the scene. If I could explain this, tear his page from
the book of telluric heart, I could understand the way victim and writing
exist side-by-side in his canon of self-made mandatory.

Sorrow. Police. Fire. *Twenty-seven angels from the great beyond.*

Crescent Nights

Exposition

That he invented an open wound and lived within it; that once lanced, he could not undo its exacting parameters; that he wanted to rise above the hiatus. Story telling. Considering awkward details; considering him. Condition critical and crucial, inclined towards the lack of, loss of, need

of synthesis, the eradication of shadow. Truth always contains seeds, prescient knowledge, of lies. Truth becomes its own fiction, implies all it does not implicate, pure grey light. The paradox of telling, tattling, the tale. Telling the story, the truth, he revealed the treachery of Eros, *logos, typos*.

Street vision, his diary of damnation. Our city, our silence. Lost in serrated landscapes, striations of the anomalous heart. Each of us knew parts and parcels of St. James Square. His invention. My baggage. Two and one to carry, *sweet chariot*. The home key, house key, tonic and tension

of this music in his country-angled heart. Land-locked. A hierarchy of disparate angels collapses in the pre-fabrication of his excoriant despair. Predisposed : Risk and resonance in the sheen of two with a singular point of view. (Hearts too slow for truth; too quick for lies.)

Luminous image and note, hostages of history intersect at the crossroads of art over articulation, units of geography the im

pulse

im

We feel the anguish of our dissensions, divisions, and separations.

raison d'existence.
In liquid bars of melodic light under coriander sky I gaze,
uncharted, at this ancient ritual moon.

Development

Fluid, frame beyond frame, photo / synthesis, photo graphic itinerary
opens eyes and ears to sensation, saturation, shall always return (re/state)
the claim, the source of source, resource and re/turn to you through angels
and keys and voices studded blue.   *Don't let the stars get in your eyes...*

A touch of home keys [riff] and the blues, lady live wire, stretched to
limits, the silk thread night remains in memory. Part I.   F-Sharp.   B-Flat.
Part II reveals the image bereft and adrift.   *The better to see you.*   Each
letter to free you, from A to Grief.   *...don't let the moon break your heart.*

Second part of this, hieroglyph, stripped to bone and dust, re/mains
[hands] a web of adverbial grief. Evening and the heart sets on an
impossible skyline. I, you, Juan, torn hearts. No longer the obsessive
fracturing into tiny geometric stones, basalt and granite, the erridean

cusp of light on these hands, this rock face.   Night, ray of moonlight,
slanted by cadmium and uranium tears; the marks made through angelus
by midnight need, scar territory.   It never ceases, this spiral down.
In the face of fiction, through the haze of memory, extend the shimmering

evening image carving shape and space, the filter of this shattered lens.
Juan, you cannot believe the cold white room, the cold white moon, a
symphony of light in the clean white look of it, crisp, your corrosive charm.
A Catholic holdout, hold over, in the name of the anger, the sign,

---

Numerous tribulations : We taste the bitter fruits : Fears, anxieties,

and the only choice.   The view from the window   :   Blood-drenched
reparation of stars.   Someone's whites.   Bluing now.   Celestial constraints.
He stood on these aimless ceremonies, stared down the barrel
of a kaleidoscopic night, lived on the edge of anonymity, balanced

the correct radical moment with a subterranean juncture of words.
He touched our paltry souls and gave us awry blessings, an inverse
confirmation through extreme negation.   The light, luminous weight,
moon-white familiarity through tunnel, cave, love; in the sign of blood.

Re   :   union station cross, stanzaic soul, tabled contents.   Labelled
stigmata for future reference.   The actual Pension Réal   :
One fuchsia carnation bled and pinned to the aorta within.
For the record.   Straight ahead, *suonare*,   for a change of south.

[Not a chance.]   His Mecca misplaced.   Oh, holiness, make safe
this passing derailment, these many detours, how much language holds
together affairs of the heart in transit, in spatial confusion.
Late, radio music low, my blood aching, blue moon in my mouth,

the stars in my eyes liquid, the terrific electricity of your invented smile.
My eyes won't let you go.   I miss your heart in my pocket,
your hand under my dress.   The kind of weather sorcery knows.
By violet light I thee read; damaged goods in these marginal eruptions,

blank pages where fingers play piercing melodies against
the length of endlessly empty nights.   His faceless face re/mains,
lodged in the vortex of memory and discovery.   Above the moon,
a silver lining, an open palm, a broken voice   :

---

frustrations, misunderstandings, antagonisms, death, & bereavement.

It's only over for you. I cannot arch enough. I go down to zero and wallow in stasis, know ledgers of love with ceaseless blank pages. Sleep, rest, less. Forgotten reclusion; etymology absolved. Foxtrot October, Charlie. My hat never touches his bones. Bravo Sierra. *He* lies still.

Recapitulation

Here, distilled to essence (her sense), sentence, stilled to presence,
an active voice out of the past private, a transformation, diction
aerial magic. She knows her way. She travels Air Grammatical, leaves
nothing simply to chance, drops hints at the hint of sound glanced. *Son,*
song, sanguine womb, wom/b/an [re : verse]; celebrate the fact
in the feminine re/cognition and lay claim to neither critical nor
condition of my idiolectic view, *lingua magica* of chance, of fate,
of win, place, show, my alpha (omega) bet. All-night sonata a shroud
of recollection, frame of consciousness, synchronous field of thought.

Linguistic emotion, primary utterance : Back to bones, basics.
Home key. Riffs. Re /solution. Against the text, a disembodied
subversion breaks me down; makes me up by the skin of my heart
imagining. Limitations essential or extraneous (chapter and verse)
but all matters in the matrix hotel/le unsecured against theft. All
he lacked. All I lack. [His hands.] Uncreated, caught in perilous
stars. Ceremonial predicate, old moon in new moon's arms. Key and
lock-hearted. In this, his galaxy, his hands cradle re/construction.
Code, coda, calcified. See? This period. Beyond here.

Some things cost too much, even when they're free. Light to regrief.

Bulletin from the Miami Hurricane Center

You reach a certain age and adjectives begin to lose their effectiveness.
Devastated, for example. You reach a certain point. A neon direction. Yes,
even choirgirls get the blues. And you know it. The way things go on and
on they gather. Gamble on the return of Pookie Pia Zadora, a cat myster-
iously gone missing on the eve of All Saints'. You learn direction a new
and personal way. Adjectival again. Maybe fiction writes better copy
for a broken heart; maybe the age passed. The broken heart : Its own
narrative shattered beyond recognition. Devastated.

You touch certain key elements and refrain from refrigerator magnetic
notes from the northward bound. Stick close to footprints trailing
echoes of *In nomine Patris...* ETC. Know who to go to for a good clutch
hit. Keep your hands close to your chest in the squeeze. Put your money
on Pia; odds against evens against even odder grammatical reconstructions.
Continental, you get the drift. Or drifters. Sometimes one floats through
blue air and settles into a sentence on a page. Or maybe I looked
at the wrong map too long. Nobody I know possesses a heart big enough
to wrap up the *Southeastern United States.* Maybe it occurred when
my eyes shaded streaks of sun. All I know : Beyond punctuation,
what constitutes silence.

I need you. I don't need you. I need you. And all of that jiving around.

[DEAR EX :]
At the time, I believe and in so doing, disregard skeins of blood.
Impulsive. Honour. And these attenuations. Somehow, I hear
the nervous clattering of my heart and its sinking. Possessive.
Stalk the foundation and collapse in the sound, my ears. Needles
and nails. At every level, the structure provides its own completion.
Studs, slats, staples. And the hammering. Insistent.

Heart. Ear. Tenacious. Telegraphic, almost. You remember this
woman. She turns away and the horizon flattens. Somehow, hurricane
windows no longer reassure. You wish to build. You know the way
to achieve vertical and horizontal precisions, know the way to the small
of my back. Construction lends itself to accuracy. Codes. Sound dynamic
by barriers we intuit in the quiescence of time.
[LOVE, O]

We live on separate plane/ts, in the maw of a reckless and new
age. She takes what she wants; returns nothing. Ultimate whore
of consumption. Genderised. Clearly viewed through rippled glass, I
discover her properties. Systole, diastole; discomfort, dislocation. Twenty-
first century disease. Angel and anti-angel caught in a search-lit spiral.
Bitch, she clutches my heart and exacts its lacerations. Fail, fall, fallen
through talons, my world dissociated in molecular ventricle distance.

My heart, my wildly broken heart. Anomalies go on forever, south of
moon this moment, but moving. No regrets : No regressions. I do not
know when it started again. All things configured. Fixed in static clarity.
Tethered to the shape and texture of zero, I turn inwards; the outbound
train cuts a swath through the eye of serrated tracks, the brutality of
horse power. The futility of random selection. All of that. Hang a star
over civilisation. Somebody sing "Rock-a-Bye Coffin" at its wake :

Hey, Zeus! The redemption of our bodies. We taste the bitter fruits.

From now to neverending, from the cradle to the grave...
Still moon. Full. A whiskey-drinking shape. Alpha to Delta, over and
out. Blues, a low-down kind of smile, an echo of teardrops, that good
old American style. Heart, under glass or water, I drink to the memory.
Another shattered night. Anno to Domini, it makes the key a clean fit,
a muscular contraction, an electrical response to binary energy, the vital
statistics of my horizontal existence. The way love dismembers a soul.

And Destiny, don't you miss me, miss dancing with this star-crossed
comet? Life on the axis, the bipolar alveolar created from liquid realism.
So much time. And difference. Disintegration. Anachronism. Other.
My other halved, lost forever in a skeleton key. I sit by the kitchen
window, no view but a valentine of black-velvet folds. Distilled morning,
thin light, out of focus, almost. A bowl of red apples. An imprint. Turn
back to black curtains. These moments striking memory, essential

separations / partitions. Black stopping my mind from flying out the
window. Did I believe in love, short form? Did I believe, in time?
Do you remember me at all (or much) from the moment we met?
Have you been trying to call me? All that. Spectacularly over.
Better to have loved and left than not to have hurt at all. That too.
Idea/l of perfecting faded love. Heart stopped, mouth forgotten.
Hands vise-gripped to the phantom shape of your arms. (Humilitas.)

Steal back to safety. Away from that island of abbreviation. Cryptic.
A sunset ceremonial. Verticality and a hint of night jasmine collide : ETC.
Tor. Ont. Can. One August afternoon, out of nowhere, a sight for singed
emotions. Anguished sleeveheart, an invitation to the blues.
Run. Running. Overrun. A frame where time eclipses. Anchor me,
dazzling array of heart and core, astonished liquid spirit, conflagration
of love. Travel through fingers to erupt in contraband enchantment

---

My friend, my mentor, my neverending self-immolating second sight.

of *peau de soie*.   Cannot look into eye, sight-squared, simply see.
Always lacked the gift of ascending garden blues.   Wore midnight
white conditionally, wanted only a concise expurgation of the book
concealing my need beneath his cardinal deed. I wandered
lost in the gutter, marginal life on an endless river of white.   I confess   :
Do you read me?   I pushed him into death.   He offered me his unholy
salvation.   I taught him to forget the necessity of breath.

Ribbons. Glide black silk, seams, slide feet into stiletto night. Strings.

Billie Holiday Visits The Last Resort

Hurt, the language of jasmine, the hand extended with a glistening edge.
A knife cut through Scylla to Charybdis. The scent I rise above. Miss
a beat. Lie down on drifting clouds. See the end of the line articulating
your fingers, moon split at its atomic core. Dancing under Nashville neon,

blood on blood. Miss a moment, instrumental; miss the vital decom-
posability of luna light. Lacunae. An incisive pornography, a gash smeared
to render the map of your jigsaw beyond retrieval, memory, a perfected
piece. These horrific parts : Breast. Thigh. Shopping bag. Calyces.

What I need to write I write around. How I move forward in a haphazard
way, how the broken heart on my sleeve ebbs and flows with out, and in
pouring silence, the unrecognisable words : Say *knife* or *love*. Over and
unconditional. Out and unemotional. The familiar directions.

Slender wishes and cirrus-thinning clouds cover slant sky with anonymous
colour. This, Nashville odyssey, search through memories to meaning
under moonlight splashes; your beautiful remonstrations; need, a meeting.
Hands awash, liquid remembrance. Antecedent to flesh. And ashes.

Do this in memory of memory. I want to hold your hand. I want to break
your heart. I want to remember the solace of zero, the upwardly oval
decline. I squeeze letters together because I cannot imagine otherwise.
Narrative conversation and the local colour smudged now, without you,

---

Second station. Second statement. Second-sight chance. She disap-

41

without your wild slanted libertarianism.   You recall nothing,
a consequence of zero, you erase the square box of memories,
the true untouchables. You forget to check the image of cloudburst
reflecting off Islamorada sometime around twilight.

You must remember this.   Fish still a fish. Boog Powell's on the verge
of sunset.   Your face rising icily above the houses in Telegraph Lane.
You will not return. I remember that. Each time I see the spine of *The
Garbageman* I know I know your place. Recall each prickly distraction.

---

pears around a marble corner, the last time you saw the vestal statue.

In the Mighty Jungle, The Tigers Sweep Tonight

Diamonds ain't forever anymore, less than evening,
lost on advertising. Two months' salary or more than memory,
self caught looking down South African mines, sandcastling
the finer innings, moments. Love and baseball never mixed.

Nor do I forget particular diamonds. The one you gave me
in a three-ring deal; the one Jackie Robinson came to know
intimately. Montréal on the west coast. Tim Raines his first homer
of the year. Tigers, the foot of the race, walking all over the Jays.

A colour screen hazing in this elemental energy. Always,
the eye, the hand, sun and essential circumstance of triple plays.
Dialogue : A pair of home runs. What keeps going
despite domed intentions, despite official earthquakes, heartaches.

Let us stand baseball brave against the clipper evening,
swings of that scat-impossible moment where music sirens the arc
and circumference of a circuit's validity. Field and grounder
tension through gradient blurs of looking in or out. The wild blue.

Yonder and righteous — Lions sleep tonight! — with relativity and liquid
tiger light. Strategy appears : A diagrammed analysis complete with
sacrifice bunts. Your legs ache. You want to take your arms for a walk.
You need to watch and time. You want this game to end. Slowly.

A secondary artifice. The limitations of sacrifice. Still caught leaning.

The Familiar Physics of Love

You ask him if he knows the way to your heartwood door; he replies
with apple-pie face : He knows the way, the wood beyond him :
Some doors' familiar electricity and the way familiar goes.

These days. Neither her nor their. Here nor t/here, from. The sound
of it safe. Neither these nor those, thanks. Not where I come from.
Siblings, structure, a photo *familias.*

And this voice. Its whole point. Shadowed, caressed. Beneath glazed
articulation, ordinary heart beat, secondary to the aching poise you effect to
saunter. Some voices familiar and the way things go.

A copy of a love letter. A copy of a key. Familial bondage
holds that sway : *You say one day we'll be together.* Sashay.
My brother, my brother! Lost : roped : tethered. My other

other. Where there's a wall there's a walleye; fish scaled and
synchronicity : Make the energy oceanic in its wave cycle : A woman
needs
X man. (Bicycle.) Make the spiralling moon its own kind of sense.

Focus. Bear down. Bury self in the implications of taking up a cross.

Lacunae : Luna Sea

Not as *temporare* as lacustrine, the presence of mind to mind the curves
ahead, the leading snakes and descending ladders, the swallowing whole.
An aqueous cycle, a nuclear splitting, its original sense of power, of pacific
impossibility in your atlantic grief. I sift into the zero I half expect
to drown me. Envelope, the shape I fear this moment of still civilisation.

An almost stone moment a moment ago, a patch of light where tears
cleanse, primarily human, these ladders to fission, only to discover
in the ascension, the patchworked spirit, serpent-sequestered, rung-
bound. Classical, neoclassical, or neolithic structures.   Vertical flaws.
Relax.   Enjoy the scenery.   Send me anemone if you think of me.

A patch of light. Not water but tears. Flood thorough. No Noah aboard.
Confusion say: "I could see primary colours, primarily human, the last time
composite."   Before drowning, before the prison door shut, the garden
sightlighted. Excrescence and a euphonious wail   :   When you know an
alibi or invent a direction, you claim a part of it, preferably with a window.

Let me see your beauty broken down like you would do for one you

My Heart Fell at Your Feet

Make me a myth circumscribing this twentieth-century circumstance
in which we find, not ourselves, but reflections pale under fibreglass and
strands of fiery pride. Art? Hardly. We dream perfect creations into
existence and wake to find only the shadow of these alignments. Time sets
sail in a boat of hope but cannot reach the shore of belief. Space opens out
(infinitely) aware of human limitation. Puny attempts to conquer

a continuum of mad reckoning. Measurement asserts linear foliage in the
flower of science; dry vacuum where love once bloomed in tender ambush,
subsuming a safe and reassuring geography. Make me a myth so I may
reach a level of self where word and prevailing mystery merge, in this,
the year of our need. Answers. Questions. Still we cannot utter
completion. If words no longer sustain, if stars no longer constellate

and rearrange galaxies of heart, how can this dim beating circular siren
transcend the knowledge of your hands? Particles stellar-splayed,
sustenance not manna but language. I conjugate myself for thee, thine
eyes, spirit, annihilation. Not that I left you; rather, that you made it
impossible for me to remain. Not that I bought a ticket; rather, that you
helped me board a plane. I did not glance back, did not commit

intercessions of myth, life recreation, narrative fraught with pain.
For months I carried the knowledge yet could not lift the veil of blood
severing my horror from my need to understand. I wanted to. I wanted
you. This afternoon I scour the universe for signs of who did what and
why. It begins with a look and ends with a glimpse. What matters?
I *fabricate* in broad daylight, flesh out reunions, stations, trains, cars;

---

love.   Riding on the Reading.   The idea of imaginative transport.

pull elegant evenings from a black silk hat without a second glance. What happens? Relationships. A to B. That sort of thing. All that work on an invisible precipice, a disaster area enacted through the present. Here, in the basement, fretting. The guitar's new strings give way to impossible arrangements, a rare kind of poetic cleaning, looking over noises, making flat music on the D-18, opening and closing my umbrella.

I always craved a D-28. Rarely play enough. Waiting for a train of musical thought to unravel this sharp line of pain cuts a swath through heartbreak Everglades wide, waiting for a line of sight. He waltzes in, Matilda. He plants boundaries to destroy on my skin. I remain carbon, dedicated, detached. *How I've missed you.* How? I listen quietly. When he concludes, I rise and walk to the nearest exit, through the pane of glass.

I believe caution arrives at its own conclusions — to keep from going absolutely insane. An uncouth alibi for absence, make that abscess, of thought. A basement, a board, a stiff set of strings. Suggest a barracuda. Touch luck. Knock on "Walk On By." *Today I passed you on the street.* Life produces casualties of absence and sorrow : In the station of transubstantiation : Cobra confirmation. I knew it would rain.

She feels like a new man tonight. Fall in line, diamond mine. Miss Try.

Arc of Evening

Another night heading across the arc of evening to star disappearance,
a suite of blues. Vancouver raining and I could cry. Always four in
the morning in this, his life. Maudlin, expedient, expendable. Terrible
tyranny lifting, up. Urban hermit nursing a badly broken heart. Edited
lover. Interior later. Fated, intrinsic, structured. Implicate, order.
Greetings : *Neverending love. Next time around can we make it forever?*
Pierced ears, eyes. Remote.

                Control. Cried it out, raged, enraged, ultimately
arrived at not terror — Oh, Aristotle! — but horror. Perish thoughts.
Always, the scar will shine in the night of his ragged life, salvaged only
in its subconscious will. The shine of my arrested heart, edges razed and
salvational beyond eyelight in absentia, memory pushed to its furthest
corner of limits. Drenched in the nostalgic mirage of the story, his own,
he breathes and falls. Head over heels. The latter technique. Milky way.

Moon motion. Accessible shape. Perpetual transformation. Discrete,

Moon in Heart Hiatus

Forever. Four walls, a heart without windows, a body dispossessed.
To explain personal effects : To see where hopelessness begins and circles
and ends.   Effect personae.   I focus, look away through liquid horror.
Numb. "I had to go in there," I whisper to you.   I cannot continue.
Above our heads, always, the moon sways in heart hiatus, a primeval
lullaby for effect, impersonal, distant.   Effects — personal, magical,
mythical — disappeared.   *When that evening sun goes down...*

---

soothing, a haven against sun static, a rigid blinding glare. Calumniant.

Absconding Gibbous Night

Running interference on the man I knew from far too many angles;
saw in clarity hand movements, tiny adjustments / readjustments
to something in the air — music or longing — or the minutiae of self-
meaning where alignments and realignments recur and recombine
in the distracted way he pushed despair through strands of greying hair,
gathering it in, absconding night and blackness enfolding flesh. To become.
And end. Bending. Breaking. This business of going on, gerunds and all,
this callosity. Night. Silk, black, a sheet I reach to fold, fold into, fold up,
and steal to shroud. Early signs of death, flood warning muffled by sheer
brooding line of sky beyond waterslash, treestreak, linen key haven. Skin.
One of the most rapturous chronicles of a love affair ever written.

Rapturous moon, the feminine, she comprehends circular sense and

Moon Break Heart

Dear You : You, a / the man I held in my arms in my bed for a time,
walk now in a room I do not know, can only see in my mind's eye. You,
a / the man I said love or some word to you; you said not to come
back, to come to you, a / the man. Ever. I know ever.

Never. Me, a / the woman you had, often, every so often always,
left often alone, knew some words, learned your language, ate it along
with other scars : *Black, waxed, death, haven, dance, siren.* Gifts to me.
I think I thank/ed you. I carry my heart under my arms; it holds

these / those words. And alone. Chant, I think. Songs. Order. Us,
one by one, not an *a / the.* Two of the blind, two of a cross. Wire.
I contain, fold in, narrow to tolerable. And cannot even wrap
my tongue around *tolerable* because it states so huge a hole in my

heart, blood, flesh. Speak. I think Ariadne and Strauss and we,
the women, strand on strand, these desert islands. No names. No place.
World spun new through grief; heart breathing again. Ah, dying?
You cross your heart and hope for rest? Not this quite green shape, this

elementary apple, gift of generous moon. Thank lucky stars, Cassandra,
heart still works, beats, cores. Pared, knife, sight stars from local point,
focal locus. Slash, I enter the blade of love, you, a / the trick knife, cause
apprehensive; defective. Damaged goods. Undeniably Yours : Love Me.

---

sun's masculine chronicles of occlusion. Over the moon, Desperado.

Man
in the Moon

I know you now; know the photographic inquisition reveals the true state
of my heart, the evidence speaks for itself, eloquently. I know you will
plough through the remainder of your days and nights with the seeds
of an open secret. I know you know; damage irrevocable, years scraped
from my eyes. Shaved from my life : So much sawdust in a big boy's
world. So much prevarication. You leave me in a circle of filings,
splinters and shards, seeking the soul of a new generation, holding reins
of restraint. Keep counsel, o-rodeo-do. Reverse video. Audio negative.

No matter the angle the reflection horrifies. Keep on walking. Don't look
now, down. I don't look back, cannot forgive. Nor unearth the place
of amnesty this time around. And wonder at that. All my life : This
lesson : You only make a difference when you don't. Matter. Spirituality.
The technohurt a stainless-steel blow. *Lingua Metallica.* The Analysis
of Technique : You do it this way : *Make sure she really needs you.*

Expunge your sister's keeper. A comprehensive sweep of knowledge about
nothing in particular, except maybe the fact I loved you,
*in my deceptive and manipulative heart, unpopulated with warmth
and human exchange* — Damn it, scarlet! — *or interchange. I scraped and
skinned my way through life, used everyone, gave nothing but a hound-
dog in return.* Never cared. Never cried. Never ran a barricade for you.

"No more hero[e]s, no more victims to immolate, no more plot. An

The lights are on, but no one's home.   You put your voice on hold, verticals;
you wrap your heart with pacemaker wishes and tissued dreams. You
understand the implications of a slap in the face. Off-centre, you level and
plumb new depths. The impact a stunning reminder to steer clear of
stationary objects; give a wide berth to falling stars. Express purpose.
Eight items or less. He thinks therefore he sinks. [Refuse to believe any
one man, regardless of thought or crime, can affect the outbreak of moon
madness, sere acuity, the diligence between *she / me* and *her / hymn*.]

Sometimes, I don't know what to think nor how to articulate the profoundly
offensive thing :   Fact in itself. I recoil from the edge
of a page and turn into the blade of the razor. She, part and parcel of me,
reclines on scaffolding of civilisation's lust without end, Amen.
Her inventor sends me *erotica*; I break into tears; I break the barrier
between woman and woman.

Somehow, Juan's need to judge and participate strangled him
before he received a special dispensation from the editor
of *Pornographic Passion Pix*. Some unguardian one or
guide let him run amok; turned away from the obscene need
in his eyes.   He took his walking papers seriously; never believed
homo sapiens could really deny him the end. Four on the floor.
The other lost.   The one he wrote under his right eye. She looks
irresistibly good by the light so French of the moon. Something
clicks. Another body down in the city tonight; another soul fluttering
recklessly from time through space seeking safe refuge, harbour,
the perpetrator of violence :   *Ciseaux, le couteau de la connaisance.*
She looks.   She sees.   She knows the death you conceal in a shopping bag.

$$LO + VE = ƎV + O⅃$$

---

immense calm...   I make discoveries through language.   Through lang-

Each morning.   Reflecting backwards, it makes a kind of sideways sense.

No indication he intends to suggest mirroring love cataclysmic;

no signal I would resist its inclusion for the duration.   We cut things;

we do this.   From nails to grass, we constantly trim and sculpt our slattern

hearts.   Each night.   Projecting mysteriously, it makes a kind of protective

suicidal sense.   *I'm not the man I think I am.*   Could I meet you above

Captain Tony's?   Could you promise always to never break this woman?

And it's wonderful now.   *I don't hurt anymore.*   Or less.   Not much.

---

uage I open myself... " Eye open.   Ear tuned to southern core textual.

Midnight Special

Noon, Friday, 52° F, 44° N. Time Passes. Tweny [sic] inches of many.
Pieces of eight separate. Monkey, you miss me yet? Temperature and
shoe shine, time and snake oil. Burning the midnight rose, the velocity of
music. I send you letters, my eight and only, my latitudinal under.

You know the mirage of mirrors, the particular atomic structures clustering
towards a stilling of self. You learn the hard way. Sometimes, you know
much too matter to distinguish between attitude and analysis, chaos and
oasis, Zen and Zed. *You pack your bags and call it* des/ti/nation.

Chaos. *I guess it doesn't matter anymore.* Or any more. I run red lights
in a complete blur. Fail to come to a full stop. Completely exhaust reasons
why the Gulf of Mexico will never know a bridge. Similar projective
completions. Tongue [un] tied : The science of silence.

I dissolve borders.   Oasis.   Evening the sound of it.
Tropical anima, heat-searing blossoms of night. The way these vowels
slide into lush foliage, travel sibilant terrain.   Neither liquid nor solid lie.
Simply a frond, a petal, asterisk. We all take chances. Foxtrot echoes.

I b r e a k down the continental divide. *It takes two takes to tango.*
Who — Dancing Under A Nashville Spell — could resist? Besides, given
the given, the street paved with palmettoes, who would want it otherwise?
A whole continent shifts through my bravo view of neverending you.

He stood at the screen, imprinted against the moon glow, hulking in

I bless the bilateral, believe bilabial, blossom in the bichimeral of the feminine. In other words, my other, I approximate square □ evenings, appropriate everything under the sun, first person singular, her feminence, far countenance. Sun burns. □ Moon glows. □ Need I speech more than?

Length of Sunday stretches across endless options of anything — *I'm going to sit right down and write myself a letter.* — A okay. Amnesia of Z. If you keep the thread scissor-cut, you pull it through the eye of your heart with half the resistance. If you take the back streets, you can make it out of the woods. You   can   drift   your   life   away.

I'll Tennessee you in my dreams. I already do. If you recall, I dreamed you and me into recollection. We touched a few chords, but couldn't take the breaks. Not a gambling town, Nashville, not a black-jacker's heaven. South of the border, but the border always changes : Dayton. Cleveland. White Garters. Toronto. And Buffalo. The Exit-53 Buffalo Motor Lodge.

We found it but we never did quite see the same map or drive the same way. I always relinquish cutlery : Knives, pistol-shaped; forks, chthonic. Border due south of this left hand. No passport. No identity. Sentimental journey through a diamond mine/d. Odd artifacts against orderly and well-executed ways of snuffing out women.   Baby, do you read me?

The thing about knowing the places, keeping their context under wraps, buttoning a lip unto the hereafter. Or maybe discretion, its own kind of silence, its judicious choice of words.   Forgive me.   I committed indiscretions. I revelled in the liquid chaos of your dangerous hands, reclined in the crook of your treacherous arms. I kissed extinction hello.

---

his undershorts, took a deep exhaustive breath and let it out through

Night. The haunting moon full. Over my shoulder. An autumnal eclipse of Titanium White by Egg-Yolk Yellow. Outline of a memory, in line with two names on the eclipse of colour. Shadow. The line about vanishing; the stage in semi-darkness. The lady did. The landlord did not. She plucked her eyebrows; he gouged her eyes. A monstrous monologue.

I read obsessively, the calibrations record atmospheric variations in valence, vector, velocity. *I can't turn the tide when it's going out on me.* Let me slide up next to you at the bar of your choice. Enough to touch base, to turn the sapphire air definitive. Gulf of Mexico. Any place you name. Include the blue/s, darling : The Sadness of the Century. (*Good*

soldiers. The ultimate good luck.) Remember the cadence of loss. Let me slide this under your doormat : The key to my Hotel Hurricane door. Do I mean *sidle*? Not in this life. Our love took off, a rocket, didn't we? Simply connected. The heart of the matter, the matter of the heart. Yours truly, with suspended sentence (or breath). How you believe

me beautiful with my mouth shut. How I mock your habit of speaking reasonably, of talking to no one in particular, particular hand in place. I believe, erroneously, in depth soundings, in knowing the lay of the land beforehand. *I'd be better off in a pine box on a slow train back to Georgia.* Or that midnight one. Check. No rocket fuel. Mate.

Pull up a chair and make yourself my own. Tell me your weather : The heat, the cold. Give me a synopsis of our fated love; show me where I sign up for relief. It hurts to keep me in suspense. Teach me you love me, help me learn the proper pronunciation of grief. An island, a strand of moon-light, flickering heat lightning. I still live in the woods.

---

the matrix wires, allowing the emptiness to inhabit him and for an

What can I possibly say?   You choose a road; it takes its toll.
You romanticise New York, the state of mind.   You wish the blues ended
in Buffalo. Or Niagara Falls. *The Rainbow Bridge Jazz & Java Club.*   Sultry
evenings swimming in liquid heat. Alive, each neuron of skin electrified
with wanting you.   Why it made a difference; why you left a mark.

Territorial evidence.   Above the border, my one below, I stumble
through horizons to unearth a map of you. You lie due south, straight drop
in the terrestrial bucket. *You never close your eyes anymore...*
You want to live in paradise without me. You want to pay the going
price. *Next time around, can we make it forever?*

Your heart, a clever bird.   Temptation a matter of feathers.   In principle,
interest, practice :   Anything you say, say yes, simply.   When does "next
time" roll around this time?   Love in the twenty-first century.   Fine
oxymoron.   No simile conveys its stainless-steel proportions; no imagery
exists. You must remember this : *It ain't cool to be crazy about you.*

Let me tell you a secret.   I receive azaleas.   Knowledge of nomenclature
associational and direct.   No angular distance on a meridian between my
livingroom window and your patio door. Or no difference. A story of
continental proportions. I put the flower pot on the coldest window ledge.
Watched Winter through deteriorating blossoms of silence.   Pungent decay.

Turning now, to Spring. I notice the green air in the thick of thickness, of
things.   Sit at the dining-area table in the basement apartment steps from
McDougall & Brown, Funeral Directors.   Since departed. Sit thinking about
body bags, pine boxes, formaldehyde. The works. Listening to *Storms of
Life*, looking at the back door with eyes from the other side of hurricane.

---

airy moment release his mind to everything.   "Love Has No Pride."

Shine a Light on Me, Operator : *Get Me Jesus on the Line*

Hurricane. (You say *hearicane*.)   I listen for the absence of weather
in your hands.   You swath yourself in inclements.   Remember the flight
you booked to Miami, its pages? We almost took off together. On the other
hand, we managed to perfect crash landings, managed to walk away
with a few minor scratches, scribblings, half-notes. Nothing broken,
nothing burned. When does hurricane season end?

The storms of life are washing me away.   Where does the lie end, the line
begin? Or vice versa. My only other. Substance and a cigarette. Nothing
else comes close. *I've been sitting alone digging up bones.* I fall through
a note in the song. I stand in the calm of the eye. *There's no place like
home.*   Heat factor. The interminable heart of languid light. Do you know
how to speak our language? Conspicuous aberration. Pack my thoughts in
order; handle with care. You move. You believe insurance will save you.
Dominus vobiscum. I determine the relative distance between your mouth
and my thighs. Temporarily blue when its particles cover you.

Or unnecessarily.   Don't get the idea. It works with barometric pressure.
Similar instruments of measurement. If you handed it to me on a ten-foot
silver platter : I wouldn't touch it. Contents under. Let me tell you
about form. The finishing nail of it. Finished, but not fishing, water,
Gloucester. You hit it on the head. Come headlong into any old time.
No such vocabularly inappropriate jargon, or variations on a juggling
theme. Don't tell me! *form is never more than an extension of content*
anymore. First, the passive shoulders the responsibility of passage.
Second, form never did rank *never more than.* Extension? Cord. Knot.
Of course not. Could not. To which building, construction? Zone and
content notwithstanding. Think of form : Question? Answer. (Two rings.)

Vers Projective : *Always wanting you but never having you, makes it*

Parallel arc of nothingness.   Sartre writes "Why Write?" in 1949.   Because Olson reads it, the existential experimentalist reinvents a need for pro-jective (cf. projectilliant / submarined / oblivious) verses based on erroneous assumptions, on the kind of platform collapsing beneath you. Take a premise.   Something to do with a collision course, with private souls and public walls.   I know rain, no stranger to precipitous shelter.   In the name of the subjective, I object.   And, it never extends itself for itself/lex. We arrive at this fork in the middle of the knife, a night, a stainless-steel desert.   Run for cover.   Form discovers content; content discovers form. A pedagogical somersault perfected through the ex-hypothesis of your insistence content somehow dominates form in your diction area, where you came form.   Charles, you hit the right formula, from Heisenberg to certain uncertainties, but your premise does not hold heavy water.   Sorry. Wrong atomic number.   Put one in the loss column.   Put two in sealed subjectivity.   A trilogy times factitious logic.   Put down that hurricane envelope.   And forget, forget the five-legged chair if only you would visit. No future in past living; no presents either.   Simply tense, all or nothing, a hit or a miss.   This life or next?   Under the umbrella of your eyes.

Under western skies.   *Maybe I'll write a book and call it* "The Blues in Black & White."   Begin a sentence with a simile, the futility of my linguistic incarceration, journey into fields of *il pleut* perfect.   Like years erased in the shattering, like none the less, like never.   Immense swallowing hangs in the air, sentenced to personal division, tables of multiplication.   Maudlin mathematical.   Refuge and constant refugee.   I go blank with wanting you.

---

hard to face tomorrow because I know I'll wake up wanting you again.

Don't care. Can't cry. Won't feel. I break insurmountable facsimiles of absolution. My hair falls out. I believe in nothing. Pyrotechnics of linguistic virtuosity, language's smoke-screen effects. Everybody causes. *Everybody knows the way I'm feeling; everybody's had the blues.* (All the semioticians cannot duplicate, deconstruct its linguistic implications. The place where a generation of scholars gathers to discuss the limitations of communion.) Put simply? The Real Presence. Radical placement. Language's light molecular. Wait until the cowboy comes home. *Always loving you; never touching you; sometimes hurts me more than I can stand.*

I can stand a lot. Can wear your memory embedded in flesh, a slash of scar and reverence. Still possess *relica amor mortu.* We begin with hurricane silence and pull into twin fiddles, pedal steel, a stray grace note, a blue left shoe. You can always count on me to count on you. You can always learn absolutely fresh ways of saying nothingness, eloquently. Take lessons from a French waiter, pick a number, stand in line. At the sound of the tone. Have a nice day. [No thanks, I have other plans.] I write against reason and passion, truth and beauty, better and worse. Juan, glance over my shoulder. Woman, the hand at my throat black-leather gloved, an obscene movement on a slow-windowing train. You never forget these things, sensations, irrational transferences. *Is it still over? Are we still through? Since my phone still ain't ringing, I assume it still ain't you.*

Station to station to saturation. *I don't need to be forgiven for loving*

That lie hammers the truth into alibi shape, hits a note squared into bull's eye. *Darling, I can't live without you and I don't know why I try; some nights I wait for morning; some mornings I break right down and cry.* I know the difference between Juan and Jesus. If only. If only I really. If only I really knew where. If only I really knew where to start, to submerge myself in beatification and emerge a hagiographic spray of spectacular wings, a fiesta of feathers del Casa Mañana. *I'd be flying home to you.* Maybe May means mañana? Maybe tomorrow I will will the disembodied disembarkation. Em, prefixial. Phonemic. Phenom. Sue, do I hear you too? Remember Sappho. All this linguistic silence. Pure science of soul's study. (Or fallout shelter.) Decrescendo. Words. Ravage & ravish. Sounds similar. Hurts familiar. Teach me another way.

One day, you sit beneath C O N L E C H sipping *café au lait,* lightning. Split in two. Yes, you know how that can happen. You never saw her before in your life. Why now? You don't even like gardenias. You think you know the ups and downs, lefts and rights, eithers and neither nors. Some one offers to learn you into existence. You know you can only offer resistance : Valence, an adverb, a handful of dead current. You install locks; each and every word hinges in the door. You believe in the father, the son, the holy parasitic ghost. You believe in McNally's map of the world; others may collapse in the gaps and gullies of Rand's impossible atlas, a cruciformly one-night hovel. The problem with a plot : You know the romance, *la vie humaine,* roman à clef, treble. Trembling and fear of noman's business. You think about every sleazy novel, how you wound up standing the night on its head, how you read every Sam or Jetflot. Home sounds vacant; love sounds a hollow lot. You could write a book; call it "A Hard Act to Follow." Uniformly, I improve. My feet rarely hurt; I resume haphazard existence in typically haphazardous ways. Keep an ear open for adjectives and adverbs. Keep a fair distance from the purification of signs. Know to run for cover when those clouds of warning roll into your eyes.

---

you so much. It's written in the scriptures; it's written there in blood.

Hemingway, will we recover? The sun sets on Barcelona. The kind of night Spain knows in order. I'll walk you to Luxembourg Gardens. Don't forget : Brown-bag it. Extinguish her claim beyond pornography. You pull out a gypsy guitar, a plywood violin. Meet me on this lethal stretch of the imagination. You play around it most of your adult life, accept separation on its own terms, the inarticulate given. And then you take a tour of its impossible inhabitants — neither here nor there — you head for the nearest exit. Rain delays. Hit-by-pitch. The blackitude. Play-by-play. Blow-by-blow theatrification of brutal preconception. Inside the sleeve. You read the unexpurgated details on the phantasmic indelibility of India ink.   Co [mpañeros].   Inside the inside sleeve, you find these liner notes:

> It was a dark and story telephone.
> Somewhere in the distance, beyond hope's
> grave on the heather, a streak of spiked
> lightning greases the madness of illuminant
> survivors of night's intoxication, the
> uncontrollable urge to extinguish the moon
> in raw materialisation. Juan did it all. Alone.
> He knew what civilisation wanted; looked
> the other way. Later, lighter, he wanted
> what he knew. Here, in the refuse of a soul,
> a powder burn. Force /d, spark /ed, inflame /d.
> Civilisation soaks you to the skin. For him,
> for all, the novel equalled saturation. The
> telephone keeps ringing. Christ, answer it!

The sky is grey. The silence is ice. No voices are heard, no faces seen,

West of Avenue night. East of easy sorrow. I long for the strength to
believe in. No change in the weather, atmospheric pressure, no movement
on the Chattanooga challenger. Won't you shuttle me home? (Heart / Soul
caught in the reflection of Lorre Verdi.) Superimposition of stationary.
She knows the miscalculations of his intentions, faces the italicised music,
recoils in holy contempt. Of the wounds of the blood of the body of this
tarnished chalice. Eucharist. She may call your entire existence into a
backward glance. The meaning of look, Sartre. Or crustaceous life.
Maybe marina; maybe mirabella; maybe a vessel of vague, gloss of vogue.

The goddamned fall. No hands. Nothing short of divine decomposition,
the failure of your heart. You only intuit the place where your hands
begin and the nails conclude, incognito. You guard against failing to beat
out the count. Down and dirty, salvation. A kiss planted in the desert
below my right eye. Ace in the hiatus, black sky. Deal me in, my late
great author of slate. Close cover before striking : A book of mismatches.
Reductio, condensed to revitalised statistics. Birth, brutality, contempt.
All civilisations make much ado about nothingness. The once-over-lightly
operatic finale to t/his glacial age.

What will you do with the remainder of your days and nights without me?
I break down in the left hemisphere of your heart, your shadow.
Trembling in sultry anticipation, travelling telaesthetic valleys and
neurasthenic mountains; your darkening blue eyes turn dazzling acts of
sadness into remnants of shredded passion. Reverence. Life on
Heartbreak Hill. Light on your face, that way, I could almost forget history
and geography, in that order. *But I cried a river, a river for him,*
that's deeper and wider than I'll ever swim. The heart it will harden;
the sorrow will dim. But I cried a river, a river for him.

---

no windows open. Frenzied hands tear at my heart. Glistening. Iced.

Radiant Intervention

You provide me with focus, nucleus, circumspection. From core to
occlusion, from apple to art. I structure these configurations of sound
into a singular voice in mind. Anyway, how do you keep need discrete,
independent, something beyond its fact-of-itself? Exigencies again.
Nothing matters more than less. Lost in a time warped by time, longing
over long distances, silences between you and me. I know your number
by heart. Always will, Atlantic. I know I shall never see you again.

We both know it. Ingrained by the time you spoke my name. August
night. The shadow again. Chiaroscuro. Warm grey light, winter-skied.
Too late, now. I undress with rigorous abandon. I turn and catch
a glimpse of our demise in the way you snuff out a candle. I cover my
ears, see you rise from the ashes of our collaborative sins of omission.
Phantom, I stalk you, walk you to the extreme borders of night's unusually
radiant intervention. You cannot call me softly, softly enough.

I imagine the sad extent of your absence in my hands. Another day, an
other desire, another space to fill. Who said obsession equals oppression?
Did you get an address? Make a commitment? Not a lot to report : I
heard the F-150 finally collapsed and died. At one time, any news
constituted celebration. Dramatic irony. Sympathetic agony. And you.
Simply an ecstasy. So what? A slob's as good as any other to a public
whore at a private trough. Drifting back. This horizontal sickness unto.

Some of us choose a linguistic set of circumstances; some of us choose a
narrative surrealism; some of us go missing. Life on the parameters of
poetic conversation, an attempt to assimilate an overwhelming mountain
of raw nervousness, the data of chaos. I never dreamed I would lean over
this dining-area table in a rented basement apartment and hold counsel
with a private alphabet, with the striations and conclusions of finitude,
point-blank range of page, point-blank over / other.

If I could pray... If you want me to beg... I'd fall down on my knees...

Harmony of Moonlight

I watch my plane ascend towards the jagged moon suspended
in its rectangular frame; west by mere degrees, the smouldering Ever-
glades reminding me of a card, a relic signed and seared with phrases
from a permanent island of temporary refuge. "Neverending Love."
A flourishing epiphany inscribed on a page from the book of my heart.
I don't know. I believe I absorb you through my fingers until you tear
my future from the socket of your everlasting past. I remove a strand
of wool you pull over my neatly structured, sadly chaotic complimentary
closing. Yours unconditionally, indestructibly. The upside oblong view
of life above the Tropic of Cancer, trans/parallelogram, latitude of love.
I could not begin at the beginning at the best of times. Now, crenelated
indanthrone blue and carmine interplay south of this acute juncture
of flight. Yours infinitively, with various shades of chromium cerulean hue,
Everglades dissolving in a frame of smoke-red lead. A heart burns up
the atmosphere. The atmospheric camarilla. Infinitesimally yours,
chronicles rapturous and wild.

I'd give anything – "... my body is enraptured ..." *– to see you again.*

Zeliotropic

The dozenth of August, does not matter, moon over milestone, a bouquet
of dust. Banquet of bereavement, hunger of loss. Under again. Drowning.
Heat wave strikes lightning out of its lexicon, scratches mandarin sky, drips
petals of succulent flesh into the thirst of my hands. *Drink to me only with
thine eyes...* I tried to walk the straight and narrow, to prove my
intoxication with desire did not extend to mere absence. Past, now. Over.

Take the A-to-Zed train to the end of the line and back. Stop over
in the refuge of love, sciamachia. Carry nothing of value across the border
of night's extenuation. Consider yourself transitory, shadowface; welcome
to zeliotropical answers to your distance-defying distractions. Struck and
stilled. The way to bring a telegram up short : of breath, of the vise
and grip of death. Western Union : So long, *sayonara*, good luck.

Note : *...the room / one narrow world / that might be anywhere...*

PHOTO: AVRUM FENSON

Judith Fitzgerald is the author of over twelve books
of poetry. She is an editor, song-writer, and
award-winning journalist who lives in Toronto.